PULPIT COVERED IN BLOOD

RECOVERING FROM A BLEEDING PASTOR

JOSHUA OKPARA

CONTENTS

Introduction --- v
Signs of a Bleeding Pulpit -------------------------------- 1
Finding the Knife -- 3
The Knife in the Leaders' Hands ----------------------- 5
   The Knife of Silence ----------------------------------- 6
   The Knife of Unbalance ----------------------------- 14
   The Knife of Financial Illiteracy -------------------- 24
   The Knife of Biblical Illiteracy --------------------- 26
   The Knife of No Vision ------------------------------ 28
   The Knife of Wrong Position ----------------------- 38
The Knife in the Pews ------------------------------------ 47
   The Knife of Sin -- 48
   The Knife of Pride and Entitlement --------------- 49
   The Knife of Immaturity --------------------------- 51
Steps Towards Healing ----------------------------------- 57
   Personal Approach- Pastors and Leaders ---------- 58
   Corporate Response ------------------------------- 62
Resources for Churches/Pastors ----------------------- 69
About the Author -- 71

INTRODUCTION

If you are well-acquainted with the church or have spent a significant amount of time within its walls, you've likely come across the phrase, "He or she is bleeding on the people." This expression is often used to characterize a preacher's motives in their sermons or their style of leadership. It carries a negative connotation, raising questions about both the preacher's intent and the message they deliver. A bleeding pulpit, by itself, cannot bleed. If there's blood spilling, it's a clear sign that the person behind the pulpit is the one experiencing the bleed.

A bleeding pastor begets a bleeding pulpit. When the pulpit is covered in blood, the words that flow from it aren't pure; they're tainted with the preacher's personal struggles and pain. The result? Congregants will leave the church feeling offended, or the preached word will fail to have a meaningful impact on their lives. I was peacefully asleep when the Holy Spirit abruptly roused me and delivered a powerful message: restoration is coming to the church whose pulpit is covered in blood. This book is precisely dedicated to that purpose— restoration. How does one recover from a pastor who is bleeding or a pulpit stained with the weight of their struggles?

SIGNS OF
A BLEEDING PULPIT

Does your church have a bleeding pulpit? Often, we associate a bleeding pulpit with pastors or preachers who come across as "very aggressive" or those who seem to emphasize their personal agenda more than God's. While there may be some truth in these observations, it's not always the whole story. The aggression we perceive can sometimes be a misinterpretation of their passion for God's Word. In other cases, preachers may inadvertently share their own opinions due to ignorance or lack of training.

There are telltale signs that may indicate your church has a bleeding pulpit. Bleeding, in the physical sense, is a sign that a wound is present or has occurred. If there's a bleeding pulpit, it signifies a bleeding pastor and, commonly, we criticize the pastor who's bleeding without addressing the fact that the blood is an indicator that a cut happened or is happening. This begs the question: who had the knife?

FINDING THE KNIFE

The "knife" is symbolic of the "why" behind the "what."

To truly comprehend a leader's actions and fruits, you must delve into the roots. Why are they doing what they're doing? The "what" may pertain to their leadership style, preaching style, or character, which could result in a diagnosis of bleeding. However, the "why" addresses the root issue, which, when addressed, can prevent the "what" from recurring. From this point on, we'll refer to the "why" as the knife that caused the bleeding.

Pain has a profound ability to challenge our theology and influence our character. Regardless of how anointed you are, pain can shape your self-perception, your view of the people you are called to serve, and even your relationship with God.

What do you do when the pain of your calling becomes unbearable and your role doesn't allow you the freedom to address the root of that pain?

Pain is indeed challenging, and the pain I'm speaking of here is the result of the knife cut. Many knives cut deep into the souls of leaders and, too frequently, proper healing is neglected, leading to continued bleeding.

To address the church with a bleeding pulpit properly, I must first emphasize that a wound exists or is forming, and a knife is involved. This prompts the question: who wields the knife?

Just as in our everyday lives, where we can be susceptible to injury, we have the potential to be cut by someone or even to cut ourselves. What do you do when the pastor is the one holding the knife? How do you address a church if its members or leadership team have the knife, causing the bleeding? We will divide the next section into two parts to address this issue: part one, the knife in the leaders' hands, and part two, the knife in the congregants' hands.

THE KNIFE IN THE LEADERS' HANDS

The knife in the leaders' hands symbolizes self-inflicted pain, whether intentional or accidental. The injury is not caused by the congregation, but rather forced upon themselves through neglect or deliberate self-harm.

A leader can inflict harm in many ways, intentionally or unintentionally, leading to them bleeding on the congregation. The specific ways this harm occurs can vary from one leader to another, but I'd like to address a few common knives that are utilized in self-inflicted cuts by leaders.

Joshua Okpara

The Knife of Silence

The knife of silence symbolizes unspoken truths, a lack of vulnerability, and unresolved issues left unattended for far too long.

This knife becomes sharper as leaders leave issues unresolved and allow their concealed frustrations to fester until they can no longer contain them, resulting in self-inflicted wounds and bleeding. This can manifest as subliminal messages or unprovoked outbursts.

Leading is challenging, and church leadership is even more demanding. Dealing with individuals from diverse backgrounds with varying personalities and opinions about how you should carry out your calling can be overwhelming. Conflicts and disagreements are inevitable, and they can be deeply frustrating. When these issues remain unaddressed and are allowed to fester, a pattern emerges. If this pattern remains unattended, cuts start to occur and the pulpit becomes tainted with blood.

To effectively lead, we must take away the knife of silence from the pastors' hands, and this responsibility falls on both the church and the pastors.

For the Church

Pastors must have a space where they can express their concerns about the church. The church should be emotionally intelligent enough to trust the pastor's heart, even when they don't fully understand their words. They should approach every concern raised by the pastor without bias, but with the perspective of being one body under Christ and with the shared goal of advancing the church.

For the Pastor

Recognizing that silence won't bring about change is the first step to speaking up. Don't allow situations and issues to fester in your heart to the point where they cloud your view of the people. Create a culture that encourages people to express their views and concerns, whether openly or anonymously, and grant yourself the freedom to do the same in a way that builds up the church.

Healing Strategy

Hey Pastor, you need a pastor too. You need a community too.

Growing up, I loved watching DC Comics, and my favorite character was Superman. He appeared virtually indestructible, yet he had one weakness— kryptonite.

Superman was one man, but he played two distinct roles in the public eye. One was Clark Kent, an ordinary individual with an everyday job like everyone else. He wasn't the first person you'd think of if a building was burning. He was just a regular man, but when he donned his costume, he transformed into Superman. With his costume on, he was no longer Clark Kent. He became the person everyone turned to for solutions to their problems.

As a pastor, you are one person with two roles and two distinct personas perceived differently depending on your environment. In a community where you aren't known, the expectations for you would differ significantly from those in a community where your calling is recognized.

In an unfamiliar community, you're akin to Clark Kent, an ordinary individual. Yet, in a community where your calling is acknowledged, you are seen as Superman, the go-to person for everything.

Unlike Superman, there is no disguise you can don in our small world; however, communities can be created where your humanity is anticipated and valued more than your status as a 'superhuman.'

You have the power and ability to create that community— a place where your soul can find support— and expectations can be set at a human level. This community thrives on transparency. You need a space to vent, to speak up, and to express yourself. Whether it's a pastor who mentors you, a counselor, a therapist, a life coach or just a friend, you need a community that values YOU more than your calling. You need a place where you can be Clark Kent, where you can receive guidance, share your burdens, and freely express your frustrations.

Questions for Reflection

For the Pastor:

1. Who pastors you?

2. Do you have a close personal relationship with that person?

3. Who are the top three people in your community that value you more than your calling?

4. Do you have a therapist? Why or why not?

Joshua Okpara

The Knife of Unbalance

The knife of unbalance symbolizes a life marked by mismanagement of time. It results from a misalignment in the time devoted to the calling and the time away from it. Either too much time is spent at the church or not enough.

The knife of unbalance is one of the most lethal weapons used to wound a ministry leader, often leading to the bloodiest of pulpits. This tool of the enemy is often misinterpreted as a sign of honor in God's eyes.

Spending too much time at the church and not enough time at home, with family, or on other responsibilities.

Far too often, ministers become wedded to the church, causing health issues, disease, and strained relationships all under the guise of "doing it for God." This trend often results in ministers losing their marriage with their spouse while maintaining an unhealthy "marriage" with the church.

Exceptional pastors may end up being terrible fathers, mothers, husbands, or wives due to this imbalance. The neglect of their families results in their children being the most neglected, leading to "preacher's kids" habitually bearing the burden of rebellion against everything related to Christendom. To some, rest is viewed as something to be enjoyed in heaven or after death. They lead restless lives, continually wounded by the knife of unbalance, which ultimately leads them to bleed on the people.

An unbalanced leader gradually evolves into a restless leader, then into a control freak who believes that nothing can function without them, locking themselves into a calling that was meant to be flexible.

As a leader, you were never called to marry the church. You are a part of the church, assigned to edify God's people. You, along with the other members of the body, are God's bride. You cannot be married to both the church and Christ at the same time.

Spending too little time at the church.

On the other hand, some leaders spend insufficient time with the church, treating it as a side gig. They abandon their calling, allowing wolves to infiltrate the flock. This imbalance results in a misguided, confused, and scattered congregation that lacks a connection with their shepherd.

This disconnect between the pulpit and the pews leads to further division among the congregation. The issue isn't whether the minister is called or not. Most likely, it's the result of an unbalanced and indecisive approach to leading according to God's pattern.

You cannot call yourself a good shepherd if you don't smell like sheep. A healthy balance of discipleship, sacrifice, and sabbatical is required to remove the knife of unbalance.

Healing Strategy

For the Pastor:

1. Implement a well-planned schedule for your church, whether over six months or one year, that includes a sabbatical.

2. Remember that rest is a sign of faith and trust. God rested, Jesus rested, and you should too.

3. A thriving ministry is one that can function without you. Have you trained your congregation to be self-sufficient?

4. If your answer is "no" to the question above, you may be holding the knife of unbalance, and without proper assessment and corrective action, you risk bleeding on the people.

Jesus provided such effective discipleship that he eagerly looked forward to his departure, telling his disciples, "I must go; if I stay, the Comforter will not come." He comprehended his mission and believed that, through his training and mentorship, his disciples were well-prepared to carry out even greater works in his absence.

Is your ministry equipped to operate independently of your presence? Furthermore, have you instilled a strong foundation of principles in your disciples so that your absence doesn't diminish the excellence of the church or its services, but instead empowers them to achieve even greater feats?

Questions for Reflection

For the pastor:

1. What is your perspective on sabbaticals?

Pulpit Covered in Blood

What is your viewpoint on being "married" to the church?

2. Have you adequately trained your successors?

3. Do you have a plan in place for someone to take over if something were to happen to you?

4. Have you scheduled time for breaks in your day, week, or month?

5. Is there a budget allocated for your sabbaticals?

Joshua Okpara

The Knife of Financial Literacy

One of the top five reasons why churches close their doors is a shortage of funds. If you are engaged in ministry, we can undoubtedly concur on the critical role that finances play in the sustenance of our work. Today, even as churches face closures, they remain the primary refuge for people in financial crises. As believers, we are seen as a beacon of hope in a world that appears to be fading. This expectation can be overwhelming, particularly for churches struggling to meet their own financial needs.

The way churches handle their finances serves as a testament to the glory of God. Our management practices effectively convey our message. In essence, a church operates as a kind of financial institution. People come in and contribute their resources with the expectation of receiving something in return, whether it's through the services provided or the assistance offered within their community.

According to Benkorp, an organization dedicated to collaborating with churches and their financial teams to establish and maintain accounting systems and financial management, it has been discovered that many individuals underestimate the importance of proper financial management within their church. Consequently, they fail to invest sufficient time, effort, or financial resources into managing these funds effectively. Without sound financial management, a church becomes susceptible to inadequate planning and budgeting, wasteful use of financial resources, potential fraud and embezzlement, penalties, and various other issues that can harm the ministry.

A lack of financial management and financial illiteracy are some of the primary reasons why some individuals hesitate to entrust their finances to the church. This distrust can also lead to a negative response in terms of giving within the ministry. People are less likely to contribute to leaders or churches they do not have confidence in.

The knife of financial illiteracy symbolizes the wounds that occur when proper systems are not established for managing church finances. This can result in leaders resorting to manipulative tactics to meet budgets they have not appropriately planned for, or they end up accumulating more debt for the ministry.

The good news is that the wounds inflicted by the knife of financial illiteracy can be eradicated through the creation of a system focused on the responsible stewardship of church finances.

Several organizations, non-profits, and a plethora of online resources are dedicated to assisting in this domain. Discovering the right resource for your needs hinges on conducting thorough research that aligns with your existing budget. However, it is imperative to emphasize that establishing a framework for financial stewardship plays a pivotal role in eliminating the adverse impact of financial illiteracy.

At the end, you will find a valuable list of church financial management software resources and non-profit organizations that specialize in providing support for effective financial management within your church.

The Knife of Biblical Illiteracy

A central theme woven throughout the Bible underscores the paramount importance of God's people engaging with His Word and possessing a deep knowledge of it. Bible literacy stands as the linchpin for the spiritual well-being of God's people. Their ability to flourish hinges on cherishing His Word, while their failure to do so can lead them into sin and judgment. Pastors have been bestowed with the profound privilege of expounding upon God's principles to the congregation. They are the lens through which the people perceive God. Before they encounter God, they encounter you, and before they listen to God, they listen to you. Frequently, you serve as their initial encounter with "the voice of God."

Where biblical illiteracy abounds, you may find yourself compelled to portray a God whose character does not align with His Word. Pastors should not assume that God's people are well-versed in the Bible, particularly in our diverse society where various cultures narrate different stories about our Creator. Nowadays, the term "truth" is often defined as a "fact or belief that is accepted as true." The predicament with this definition is that what a group of individuals collectively accepts as true becomes "their truth." Our world hungers for truth and the devil is acutely aware of this yearning. As a result, much of the deception in the world masquerades as the church, with wolves donning sheep's clothing.

In their quest for truth, many have fallen prey to distorted teachings, which lead them to embrace belief systems misaligned with the Word of God, thereby ensnaring them in spiritual bondage. We find ourselves in an era where the world must recognize that there is an ultimate Truth, and this Truth is not a mere fact or belief, but a person—Jesus Christ. As stated in John 14:6, Jesus is "the Way, the Truth, and the Life." Only this Truth possesses the power to liberate those in bondage. It is through a profound understanding of the Word of God that we find freedom, as articulated in John 8:32. However, how will people come to know the Truth if the preacher remains ignorant of it?

Biblical illiteracy inflicts wounds upon both the pastor and the church, tainting the Word of God with human opinions and false teachings. As pastors, we are held to a higher standard, as emphasized in 2 Timothy 2:15, which urges us to "study to show ourselves approved unto God, a workman that need not be ashamed, rightly dividing the word of truth." The sole means of halting the wounds inflicted by the knife of biblical illiteracy is to diligently study and show us approved. We must grasp that until individuals truly encounter and comprehend the Truth, they will remain ensnared.

The Knife of No Vision

Proverbs 29:18 instructs us, "Where there is no vision, the people perish: But he that keeps the law, happy is he." While the context of this scripture primarily addresses a lack of revelation regarding God's will and the consequences of a true absence of prophetic vision, the underlying principle can be applied to the concept of having a vision.

In the tangible realm, sight and vision are of utmost importance as they enable us to engage with our surroundings, ensure our safety, and maintain the sharpness of our minds. Similarly in ministry, having a vision provides direction and offers a platform for translating goals into tangible realities. Where there is no vision, it's not just the people who suffer; the ministry also languishes.

The very foundation of our Christian journey is rooted in having a vision. Our faithful service to God is driven by the knowledge that a reward awaits us. We follow His will because we understand that the current trials are incomparable to the glory that lies ahead. If there were no ultimate reward, few would serve. If you were told that serving God would lead you to eternal damnation, you would think twice.

Vision is what propels us toward eternity, and it plays an even more significant role in maintaining the earthly ministry. Without vision, confusion takes root, resulting in division. Individuals will begin to chart their own paths based on their individual perceptions of what is fitting. In the absence of vision, peace and unity dwindle, and growth becomes stunted. People don't merely contribute to a ministry, they contribute to a vision. They don't volunteer for opportunities, they volunteer for a vision. When the pastor or ministry lacks a clear sense of direction, it paves the way for chaos.

One of the fundamental advantages of having a vision is that it helps filter out those whose personal goals and ideas do not align with the ministry's overarching vision. Initially, this may be painful, but it is indispensable for the ministry's future. Casting a vision establishes expectations and ensures that objectives materialize. It also sifts out those who are misaligned with the ministry.

An illustrative example can be found in John 6:22-66 when Jesus presented a vision of the true and living bread of God, identifying Himself as that bread. This culminated into disciples who did not align with that vision turning away and ceasing walking with Him.

One effective way to address a rebellious or uncommitted crowd is by casting a clear vision. Vision unveils those who stand with you and those who do not. Nevertheless, where there is no vision, both the people and the ministry face the risk of perishing.

As a unified body, the church shares a universal vision and overarching goal, with each member playing an individual role in this grand design. Your ministry is akin to a vital body part, and the function you fulfill within the overarching vision corresponds to your personal vision for advancing God's kingdom. Leaders must diligently seek God's guidance to discover their distinct vision for the ministry they are entrusted to lead.

The knife of no vision is one that continuously prunes leaders who refuse to seek God's guidance regarding the direction of their ministry.

Questions for Reflection

For the pastor:

1. What is the overarching vision for your church?

2. To which age group and community are you specifically called to minister, and how are you effectively reaching out to them?

3. What are the prevalent needs within the community you are called to serve?

Do you possess the requisite funding and resources to address these needs adequately?

4. Have you assembled a dedicated team entrusted with carrying out this vision?

5. Could you delineate your short-term, mid-term, and long-term goals for your ministry?

6. Envision your church five, ten, or fifteen years from now. What does it look like?

Joshua Okpara

The Knife of Wrong Position

This issue poses a double-edged challenge, impacting both the pastor and the church simultaneously. While everyone is called to proclaim the gospel of the Kingdom, not all are called to assume the role of a pastor and shepherd a congregation.

In our earthly context, such as in sports, the individual recognized as the winner holds the esteemed number one position, and anyone falling short of that status is often deemed a loser. I recall hearing a lyric once that succinctly stated, "Being number two is just being the first to lose."

Our societal culture is inherently predisposed to celebrate and exalt the top-tier individuals within distinct categories. However, the dilemma with this ideology is that it does not adequately align with the principles of the Kingdom.

In the body of Christ, Jesus holds the singular position of being the ultimate number one, and every member, including pastors and leaders, forms an integral part of the body of Christ. Within this body, various roles and positions exist. Each member is assigned specific tasks and responsibilities aimed at edifying the body of Christ.

These roles come with unique duties and assignments that are accompanied by a specific equipping and anointing necessary for executing those tasks efficiently. Each role possesses a particular grace that facilitates the intended outcomes of that role. When someone operates effectively within the right position, their work may appear effortless to an observer. People may mistakenly assume that they can perform the same tasks they witness others doing. What they fail to realize is that each role is accompanied by a distinct anointing that makes it effective.

The anointing doesn't shield individuals from the challenges inherent in their roles, but it does empower them to carry out their tasks effectively.

Throughout the history of the Church, the issue of roles and positions has been a subject of continuous debate and discussion. A multitude of viewpoints and concerns can be illuminated, but for the purpose of this theme, I will spotlight three key issues that could impede unity in understanding God's perspective on roles in the Church.

First: The Elevated Status of the 5-Fold Ministry Beyond Reproach.

Within the body of Christ, God has ordained specific roles to uplift and strengthen the church. These roles encompass the Apostle, Prophet, Pastor, Evangelist, and Teacher. Each of these roles carries a unique anointing tailor-made for the individual called to operate within it. These roles essentially function as divine appointments granted by God for the betterment of the church. However, it's imperative to remember that the individuals who occupy these roles are human beings, complete with flaws, mistakes, and the ongoing need for character development just like everyone else. These individuals are integral components of the body of Christ, each assigned by God to play a distinct role in edifying the body.

An issue arises when we conflate the office and the individual, elevating the person within the office to a status above reproach. This unfortunate elevation can result in abuses and perversions of power. It's essential to recognize that even those chosen for these roles remain human, susceptible to err and requiring correction and discipleship. Elevating them to a status beyond reproach severs their connection with accountability and allows unchecked fruit to flourish.

This elevation also contributes to the problematic desire of many to attain these roles. They are not motivated by a genuine call but driven by a thirst for recognition, worship, and the desire to be held in higher esteem than others. Such unrighteous desires plant seeds of ambition, which, when matured, bear the fruit of ministries founded on perversion and vain glory.

Second: The Misconception of the Pastor/Leader as the Ultimate Number One.

While it's true that leaders bear a greater responsibility in shepherding God's flock and will be held to a higher standard by God, it does not diminish the importance of their role within the body of Christ. The pastor holds a position just as vital as the janitor or the worship leader, albeit serving different functions within the body.

The problem arises when people aspire to be the head of the church without understanding that the position of the head is already occupied by Christ Himself. This implies that the available roles are those of other body parts.

Seeing the pastor as the head of the church often leads those who regard themselves as number two to scrutinize the leader with the aim of assuming their position. When the role of the leader is not perceived as part of the greater body, it can easily become an idol within the body.

Consequently, many individuals aspire to assume the role of the pastor while neglecting the specific role they were anointed for. This misalignment results in dysfunction within the church body. Every role is significant! I was reminded of this during the COVID-19 pandemic in 2020 when our church experienced an outbreak. I came to appreciate the value of my taste buds. I lost my ability to taste food, and everything I ate resembled rubber. I marveled at how such a small part of my body could have a significant impact on my comfort. My hands and feet worked fine, but the inability to taste left me with no desire to eat, ultimately weakening my entire body. A small sensory organ affected my whole body. Likewise, within your church, roles such as door greeters, janitorial teams, music departments, media teams, hospitality teams, and more are akin to sensory organs in the body of Christ. When we recognize that we are all integral parts of one body, each role holds equal value. This perspective diminishes the yearning among congregants to be another part as everyone appreciates their unique role.

The duty of the leader is to underscore, through both actions and teachings, that they are simply a part of the body of Christ just like everyone else. This truth, when embodied and articulated, offers benefits to both the pastor and the church.

Third: The Emergence of Ministries Born Out of Disagreements with Leaders.

A concerning phenomenon observed within the sanctified pulpit is when individuals, initially designated to serve in a supporting role, establish their own ministries founded by grievances against their former leaders. This distressing course of action can lead to undesirable consequences. These individuals may subtly direct their followers with messages that implicitly criticize their previous leader, sowing discord.

Alternatively, in their zeal to set themselves apart and prove their leadership superiority, they might devise a vision that lacks divine inspiration, inadvertently steering their congregation away from God's intended path.

For those who embark on a ministerial journey fueled by unresolved conflicts with their former leaders, and who have not sought reconciliation, they inadvertently wield an authority fraught with peril, capable of nurturing rebellion among their followers.

Church divisions, often resulting in two or more separate congregations, are a painful experience for pastors and church members alike. These splits can be triggered by doctrinal disputes, scandals, hurt feelings, unspoken expectations, conflicts, miscommunications, sin, and various other factors.

The wounds stemming from these divisions cause the pulpit to bleed. If you are a pastor who initiated your ministry following a church split, reconciliation is imperative to stem the bleeding. Return and make amends so that, if you are indeed called by God, you can leave in the right manner. Many pastors are still hurting from the aftermath of church splits.

Questions for Reflection

For the Pastor:

1. What role were you originally called to fulfill within the church?

2. Does the role you were initially called to align with your current position? If not, why the change?

Ministry involves human beings. As humans are prone to making mistakes, occasional conflicts can appear inevitable. To gain a comprehensive understanding of a leader's actions and outcomes, we must delve into the underlying causes. Why do they act as they do? The "what" may refer to their leadership style, preaching method, or character, which may result in a diagnosis of "bleeding." However, the "why" delves into the root issues. By addressing these, we can prevent the "what" from recurring.

THE KNIFE
IN THE PEWS

Identifying bleeding within the pulpit while disregarding the fact that the knife may be in the pews would be unreasonable. We must confront the fact that bleeding indicates a cut has occurred or is currently taking place, and this cut could be self-inflicted or the result of actions within the congregation. We have discussed some examples of self-inflicted cuts that may lead to bleeding in the pulpit. In a similar vein, it is vital to acknowledge the wounds inflicted when the knife is in the pews.

Pain possesses the undeniable ability to challenge our theology and shape our character. Regardless of one's anointing, pain can affect how they perceive themselves, the people they are called to serve, and even their relationship with God. What should one do when this pain stems from the very individuals they are meant to serve? How should one respond when he or she is wounded, and the source of that pain lies within the congregation?

The Knife of Sin

One of the first knives that can cut the leader in the pulpit stems from sin. When I mention sin, I am referring to Ephesians 4:31, which advises us to "get rid of all bitterness, rage, anger, brawling, and slander, along with every form of malice." This encompasses gossip and any ungodly interactions. I am encompassing all these various categories under the term "sin."

One of the most disheartening things a church can do to wound its pastor is to be divided. When bitterness, rage, anger, brawling, slander, and every form of malice permeate the pews, the consequences can be devastating. Here are some of the results:

1. It wounds the leader in the pulpit, discouraging him/her and implying that the preached word is ineffective.

    Often, members may be unaware that their interactions with each other can harm the leader and hinder the ministry's growth.

2. It projects an image of the church that people sometimes blame on the leader, who may or may

not be aware of it. This can deter new membership and the overall growth of the ministry.

3. It obstructs the flow of the Holy Spirit within the church.

Where sin is present, it acts as a barrier to the Spirit's work.

It is crucial to recognize the high priority placed on maintaining peace with all people. The Bible states in Hebrews 12:14, "Strive for peace with everyone, and for the holiness without which no one will see the Lord." God places such significance on harmony in the pews that without it, we cannot witness His presence.

This verse can be understood both literally and figuratively. In Matthew 5:16, we are encouraged to "let our light shine before men so that they may see our good works and glorify our Father in heaven." In other words, people perceive God through us. If an unbeliever enters the church and encounters sin in the form of anger, bitterness, rage, brawling, slander, and malice, they lose an opportunity to encounter God.

The Knife of Pride and Entitlement

Another blade that can wound leadership in the church is the knife of entitlement and pride. When church members adopt an entitlement mentality, they often misconstrue the role of the pastor as that of a hired servant. They see leaders as individuals solely paid to focus on them and cater to their needs. In this perspective, they lose sight of the humanity of the leader and their family, and their sole focus becomes having their personal needs met.

When this entitlement mentality takes hold, it can lead to the formation of unhealthy alliances.

This mindset tends to spread rapidly among immature believers who join forces to undermine the leader and shift the church's focus from the Kingdom to their own needs. They form alliances with influential individuals within the church and actively seek out faults in their leader that can be used against them.

Entitled individuals often do not contribute to the vision, but instead see their giving as a fee paid to the church to support their self-serving behavior. They become irate when their desires are not met and may even craft a different vision from that set by the church leader.

In some cases, individuals with an entitlement mentality may operate out of ignorance, unaware that they are being used by the enemy to sow division within the church and harm the pastor.

Entitlement can creep in when unspoken expectations are not met. For instance, when someone, perhaps a family member of the pastor/leader or a prominent figure within the church, does not get their way, disappointment can result. If the issue is not communicated effectively, bitterness can take root and foster an entitlement mentality.

The Knife of Immaturity

The knife of immaturity possesses the potential to inflict severe harm. When a church member resists maturing, their immaturity becomes a seed that bears fruit in the form of various negative behaviors: lack of communication, disrespect towards leadership, excessive pride in spiritual gifts, the formation of cliques, legal disputes within the church, immorality, favoritism, and division within the church. All these behaviors create a cutting edge that deeply wounds the church leader.

It's essential to recognize that church membership does not automatically equate to being a mature Christian. Many individuals mistakenly associate their ability to articulate God's word with spiritual maturity. Immaturity is the result of hearing but not applying the word of God, indicating a lack of wisdom. It is a sign that knowledge has not been effectively translated into practice. Immaturity results in various destructive fruits.

Fruit of Gullibility: Immature believers are easily swayed by deceit and characterized by their instability. A telltale sign of an immature believer is their inability to be grounded and their tendency to move from one ministry to another.

Fruit of Offense: Immature believers are frequently offended by various matters and tend to make assumptions about others' intentions. This offense leads to a victim mentality and a perception that everyone and everything is against them.

Immature believers habitually find themselves in a perpetual state of offense, struggling to get along with others, causing conflict within the church, and promoting division while positioning themselves as victims.

Fruit of Disobedience: Immature believers struggle with obedience, regularly thriving on rebellion. They disregard church attendance, financial contributions to the vision, and fail to follow the instructions given to the church body. Their actions frequently contradict the leader's vision, and they may willingly allow themselves to be used by the enemy to foster division within the church.

Fruit of Rebellion: Rebellion represents opposition to authority and can manifest in both overt and subtle forms. It typically begins within the heart and is regarded as a sin against God and humanity. It opposes order and structure, and rebellious individuals harbor disdain for unity and community. They seek independence from the leader's vision, withdraw loyalty from the church, and frequently engage in fault-finding and deception.

The definition of rebellion is aptly expressed in 1 Samuel 15:23, "For rebellion is as the sin of witchcraft, and stubbornness is as iniquity and idolatry." It is essential for those embracing rebellion to understand that it is sin. Its source is in the devil, whose aim is to steal, kill, and destroy, as stated in John 10:10. Immediate repentance is necessary for true deliverance.

Fruit of Selfishness: Immature individuals struggle with generosity and exhibit a self-centered focus. They prioritize themselves and consider their cause to be of utmost importance. Their generosity towards the church's vision is limited, and they often express discontentment when giving is involved. They invest more in offering words and opinions concerning church finances than they do in personally contributing to the church's resources.

Healing and Deliverance Strategy

The good news is that there is a clear strategy for healing and deliverance, and it begins with repentance, a wholehearted surrender to the Holy Spirit, and a foundation of genuine love.

Immaturity can lead to sin, and the consequence of sin is death. The pathway to avoiding these consequences is through sincere repentance, involving a complete turnaround. Immature believers must turn away from their own ways and fully submit to the will of God and His indwelling Spirit. As Galatians 5:22-23 reminds us, "But the fruit of the Spirit is love, joy, peace, patience, kindness, goodness, faithfulness, gentleness, self-control; against such things, there is no law."

Those who belong to Christ have crucified the flesh with its passions and desires. It's important to identify that the desires of the flesh, as mentioned in Galatians 5:19-21, encompass works such as immaturity. To overcome this, one must entirely yield to the Spirit of God and embrace God's way, guided by love.

Love is not merely a sentiment but an active expression of genuine care and consideration. The Bible provides a concise definition of love in 1 Corinthians 13:4-7, "Love is patient and kind; love does not envy or boast; it is not arrogant or rude. It does not insist on its own way; it is not irritable or resentful; it does not rejoice at wrongdoing but rejoices with the truth. Love bears all things, believes all things, hopes all things, endures all things."

To gauge your spiritual maturity, self-evaluate based on how well your life aligns with the characteristics of the fruit of the Spirit and love. If your name were substituted for the word "love" in the verse, would it still hold true? Can it be genuinely said of you that you are patient and kind? We must allow our lives to be continually guided by the Word of God, the fruit of the Spirit, and the principle of love. Through the diligent application of God's Word, we can experience growth and maturation in our walk with Christ.

Healing Strategy: Embrace Discipleship

Submitting to discipleship: The pivotal path to authentic maturity lies in embracing discipleship. Without discipleship, genuine growth remains elusive. Members are called to mortify their flesh, recognize the vital importance of discipleship, and fully commit to the process.

Committing to discipleship entails accepting love, correction, rebuke, redirection, and teaching. It is a pledge to apply the preached Word of God in one's life earnestly. This dedicated commitment not only uproots the knife of immaturity from the church, but also paves the way for healing and unstoppable spiritual growth.

Joshua Okpara

STEPS TOWARDS HEALING

Throughout this process, it was crucial for me to acknowledge the presence of many within the church who are presently experiencing the effects of a bleeding pulpit. Simultaneously, there are pastors who find themselves in a state of internal bleeding. Identifying the root causes of this bleeding is paramount, but it's equally essential to implement effective measures to address those currently affected by the consequences of a bleeding pulpit.

So, what can you do if you're currently bearing the weight of the blood spilling from the pulpit? How can you navigate the challenges of preaching, teaching, and serving when you're constantly wounded from the pews or the pulpit?

To stem the flow of this spiritual hemorrhage and facilitate recovery, we must consider both personal and corporate approaches.

Personal Approach- Pastors and Leaders

How to Address Wounds When the Knife is in the Pews

Just as a patient seeks a doctor when injured, pastors and leaders must follow a similar approach when they are wounded by actions or attitudes within the congregation. It's essential to recognize the need for self-care and healing. Here are the steps to take when dealing with these wounds:

1. **Stop the bleeding.**

    Just as one would immediately address physical bleeding, pastors should take a break from preaching or teaching to prevent further harm to themselves and the congregation. Stepping away temporarily allows the leader to heal and prevents their emotional or spiritual struggles from affecting the congregation.

2. **Cleanse the wound.**

    Like cleaning and disinfecting a physical wound, it's crucial to address any errors, misunderstandings, or miscommunications that may have caused the bleeding within the church. Clear up any confusion or issues immediately to prevent further damage or potential harm to the congregation.

3. **Seek professional help.**

   In the same way a doctor examines and treats a physical injury, pastors and leaders need to seek guidance and support from trusted individuals. This may involve consulting with therapists, pastors, counselors, or mentors who can help identify the source of the pain and provide appropriate care. Accountability, therapy, counseling, strategy sessions, and ongoing training can help in this process.

4. **Receive covering and protection.**

   Just as every patient benefits from medical care, every pastor needs a pastor. It's important to be open to covering, discipleship, and coaching throughout the healing journey. This provides essential support and guidance as you recover.

5. **Allow time for healing.**

   Healing takes time, and there's no shame in taking a sabbatical or break to recover. When a wound is detected, and bleeding is present or imminent, a pastor should recognize the necessity of personal healing and growth for the protection and development of the church. Prioritizing your own well-being is not only beneficial for you, but also for your congregation.

Key Strategies for Implementation

1. **Foster open dialogue and therapy sessions.**

    Encourage open and honest conversations with individuals within the church to provide a safe space for them to express their concerns and grievances, allowing them to drop their metaphorical knives.

2. **Bring in a spirit-filled therapist.**

    Regularly host sessions led by a licensed therapist who is well-versed in handling emotions and interpersonal issues. These sessions can occur quarterly or semi-annually, providing the congregation with valuable emotional and spiritual guidance.

3. **Establish pulpit protection measures.**

    Ensure that the pulpit remains a safe place by implementing safeguards against potential infiltrators with harmful intentions.

a. Create a filter mechanism.

> Designate a trusted intermediary or team responsible for filtering and addressing certain issues or situations that the pastor or leader should not handle personally. Delegating effectively can help prevent unnecessary cuts.

b. Appoint ministry positions for member affairs.

> Develop specific roles within the ministry for individuals capable of handling minor tasks and addressing low-risk member concerns. This way, the congregation can access support for their needs without burdening the leader.

4. **Embrace transparency.**

Follow the example of the apostle Paul, who openly shared his struggles, weaknesses, and the challenges he faced for the sake of the gospel (2 Corinthians 11:16-33). Be transparent about your humanity as a leader. Concealing imperfections can lead to unrealistic expectations in the congregation and potential misuse or abuse. Promote authenticity to foster a healthier church environment.

Joshua Okpara

Corporate Response

When the church family or a member is victimized by the blood flowing from the pulpit, immediate and deliberate actions are required for genuine healing. Being bled on is painful and, akin to the natural world, blood can attract predators to prey. When the pulpit is tainted with blood, it not only sullies the integrity of God's word, but also draws predators to the vulnerable sheep. This bloodshed within the pews often leads to what's commonly referred to as "church hurt."

When individuals are emotionally, mentally, spiritually, or even physically wounded by leaders they once trusted, the path to recovery can be arduous. Many depart from the church and never return due to these experiences. Church leaders, being human, are susceptible to making mistakes and can struggle emotionally.

Frequently, the bleeding within the pews remains unaddressed by the leader in the pulpit because the source of the issue lies with the leadership. It can be challenging to disentangle the loving God from the misrepresentation of God by an unhealthy leader.

The first step in resolving this issue is recognizing that God abhors abuse as well. Just because the abuser holds the title of a man or woman of God does not diminish the fact that God loves and cares for His people and intensely detests abuse from the pulpit. He punishes leaders who mistreat His people, as evidenced throughout the Scriptures in cases involving leaders such as Pharaoh, David, Saul, Nebuchadnezzar, the Pharisees, and the Sadducees.

While God's judgment on abusive leaders is clear, it doesn't negate the trauma inflicted by their actions. How should the pews respond to the wounds from the pulpit?

First: Recognize the Wound and Stop the Bleeding.

Ignoring abusive leadership is one of the gravest forms of neglect. In the presence of abuse, healthy confrontation is necessary. A scriptural framework for addressing this issue can be found in Matthew 18:15-17: "If your brother sins against you, go and tell him his fault, between you and him alone. If he listens to you, you have gained your brother. But if he does not listen, take one or two others along with you, that every charge may be established by the evidence of two or three witnesses. If he refuses to listen to them, tell it to the church. And if he refuses to listen even to the church, let him be to you as a Gentile and a tax collector."

I've referred to this scripture because a pastor or leader can also be a brother or sister in Christ. The first step in addressing any issues with such an individual is to approach them in a healthy manner with the goal of seeking understanding. In my book, *Conflict Resolution*, I delve into more comprehensive techniques for handling conflicts in your personal life and relationships. It is crucial to rigorously follow the steps provided in Scripture for managing conflicts.

1. Engage in a healthy confrontation with the person, seeking understanding and leading with questions, not assumptions.

2. If there are impartial witnesses to the abuse (individuals who are genuinely neutral), involve them if the initial confrontation fails to bring resolution.

3. If the presence of witnesses still fails to lead to understanding and resolution, bring the matter before the church elders, leadership, or board.

4. If no resolution is achieved at this stage, it may be best to consider leaving that church to prevent the growth of bitterness and resentment.

Second: Seek Treatment for the Wound and Clean the Site.

1. **Seek treatment to prevent infection.**

   If you've experienced any wounds from the pulpit, it's vital to address them promptly to avoid further harm or spiritual infection. Recognize that internal healing is essential for your soul's well-being and overall spiritual growth.

2. **Seek support outside the church:**

   When the wound is inflicted from the pulpit, consider seeking support from an impartial, spirit-filled individual outside your congregation. Consult a counselor, therapist, or trusted friend who can provide guidance and a safe space for your healing journey.

3. **Foster a supportive sealing environment to gain a healthy perspective.**

   To recover and heal effectively, it's crucial to be in an environment that nurtures your emotional and spiritual well-being.one must actively pursue a healthy perspective, ideally from someone outside your specific church, to help you process your experiences and emotions. Avoid Biased Surroundings: Steer clear of situations where biased individuals may perpetuate feelings of resentment, anger, and bitterness.

4. **Embrace wholeness and prosperity.**

   Remember that God desires your wholeness and prosperity, aligning with 3 John 1:2. Your spiritual nourishment is as important as nourishing your physical body.

Third: Allow Time for Healing.

Taking a break from responsibilities to allow for healing is not a sin. Unhealed individuals cannot lead effectively. Without giving adequate time for healing, a trigger can easily reopen the wound, leading to further suffering.

Numerous members never took the time to heal, resulting in bitterness toward leadership. This bitterness then fuels negative interactions with others and church leadership, ultimately working internally to destabilize the church, deter new members from joining, and hinder the growth of the ministry. Taking time to heal is more effective than remaining in a situation where bitterness festers.

RESTORATION FOR THE PULPIT

If you're acquainted with the church environment or have been part of a congregation for some time, you may have encountered the phrase, "He/She is bleeding on the people." This phrase is used to critique a preacher's sermons or leadership style, implying a negative intent behind the delivered message. It raises questions about the authenticity of the preached word and the preacher's motives. A bleeding pulpit is a result of a bleeding preacher. It's important to note that the pulpit itself doesn't have the capacity to bleed. When blood appears to be spilling, it indicates that the individual behind the pulpit is the one experiencing the internal turmoil.

A bleeding pastor contributes to a bleeding pulpit. When the pulpit is marred with metaphorical blood, the word that emanates from it is tainted by the preacher's internal struggles. The consequence can be congregants leaving the church offended or the preached word failing to impact their lives. The presence of bleeding serves as a sign that a cut has transpired and someone holds a metaphorical knife. The pressing question is, where does this knife reside—within the pews, the pulpit, or both? Identifying the presence of blood is just the beginning.

It requires meticulous work to discover the source of the cut. Only then can we collectively embark on the path to healing as a church.

Now is the time for the church to heal and bravely address the issue of bleeding from the pulpit, ensuring that our sermons and leadership are no longer tainted with blood. May we be restored, in Jesus' name. Amen.

RESOURCES FOR CHURCHES/PASTORS

Here are some recommended resources for churches and pastors:

1. Ministry Pass: Discover 17 must-have resources for small church pastors.

   https://ministrypass.com/17-must-have-resources-for-small-church-pastors/

2. Church Source: Explore a wide range of church leadership resources.

   https://churchsource.com/pages/church-leadership

For counseling and therapy services:

Abide Leader Care: Access counseling and therapy services tailored to leaders in the church. https://www.abideleadercare.org/

https://www.biblicalcounselingcoalition.org/

Mental Health & Bible: Discover mental health and care resources relevant to your spiritual journey.

https://mentalhealth.bible/care/

ABOUT THE AUTHOR

Joshua Okpara, hailing from Lagos, Nigeria, learned the resilience required to conquer adversity at a young age. He faced the tragic loss of his mother just two weeks before his eighth birthday. Shortly thereafter, he embarked on a journey to the United States, seeking a fresh start.

Navigating the challenges of adapting to a new and unfamiliar environment, Joshua grappled with anxiety, depression, and even contemplated suicide. At the tender age of 14, he survived a suicide attempt, which marked the beginning of his mission to inspire, challenge, and motivate others to discover and live out their God-given purpose.

"Unfamiliar territory develops self-awareness."

Joshua's unwavering belief in God's blessing to humanity—as stated in Genesis 1:26, to rule the Earth in His image and likeness—serves as the driving force behind all his endeavors. This foundational belief underpins the resources he provides, his consulting and coaching work, and his ministry.

Joshua Okpara is the accomplished author of ten best-selling books, including titles like, *Where Does It Hurt? 31 Days to A Better You, Handling Uncertainty,* and *Discovering Your Value*, which have garnered international acclaim.

Joshua is married to Charmecia Okpara and, together, they are raising their son, Josiah Okpara. Recognized for his charisma, leadership, and profound dedication to purpose, he also holds the position of founder and senior pastor at Faith Filled Church, situated in Lewisville, Texas. Joshua's life and work continue to inspire and empower those around him.

www.ingramcontent.com/pod-product-compliance
Lightning Source LLC
Chambersburg PA
CBHW070742060526
44119CB00071B/116